A
Medieval
Illuminated
Book of Days

THE BRITISH LIBRARY

- o -

Museums and Galleries Marketing Ltd

Personal Information

Name

Address

Postcode/Zip

Home Telephone

Home Fax

Home Email

National Insurance/ID Number

Passport Number

Bank

Personal Information

Business Address

Postcode/Zip

Business Telephone

Business Fax

Business Email

Car Registration

Driving Licence

Emergency Contact Telephone

Blood Group

Introduction

Large numbers of superbly illuminated books of hours, the universally popular manual of private devotion, have survived from the Middle Ages and Renaissance. Among the finest is the Hastings Hours, produced in the southern Netherlands in the last quarter of the fifteenth century, from which the illustrations in this book of days are taken.

The manuscript was written and illuminated for William Lord Hastings, a close friend and loyal supporter of Edward IV of England. Its anonymous artist, who is known as the Master of the First Prayerbook of Maximilian in honour of one of his later works, was one of the foremost figures of the celebrated Ghent-Bruges school of illumination. Much of the work of these artists was carried out for members of the Burgundian ducal court, at that time including Duchess Margaret, who was Edward IV's sister. The Hastings Hours is one of the first to include illusionistic border decoration in which flowers, insects and other objects appear to float above the page, casting painted shadows on a coloured background. The delicate shades in which they are painted were carefully chosen to harmonise with the tones in the individual miniatures which they enclose.

Hastings paid many visits to the Netherlands and northern France and may well have made his choice of illuminator in person. The manuscript probably dates from the late 1470s and cannot in any case be later than June 1483 when its owner was summarily executed in the Tower of London by order of Richard III. Its later history is obscure. Almost unknown until it was bequeathed to the nation in 1968 by Mrs F W M Perrins, the Hastings Hours is now Additional MS 54782 in the collections of The British Library.

Book of Days

1

2

3

4

5

6

7

Memoria de sco ypoforo. ant

sancte ypofo
ir martiu
i ihesu ypusti
qui pro eius
noinme pe
na pertulisti: opem confer in
scris atq3 mundo tristi. qui
celestis gloue regna mariusa
ypoforii sancti speciem quicui
q3 tuetur illo nempe die nul
lo languoze grauetur: confer
solamen et mentis tolle grii
uamen. Judicis examen fac
mite sic ommbus. V. Oza
pro nobis beate martir ypo

8

9

10

11

12

13

14

15

16

17

18

19

20

21

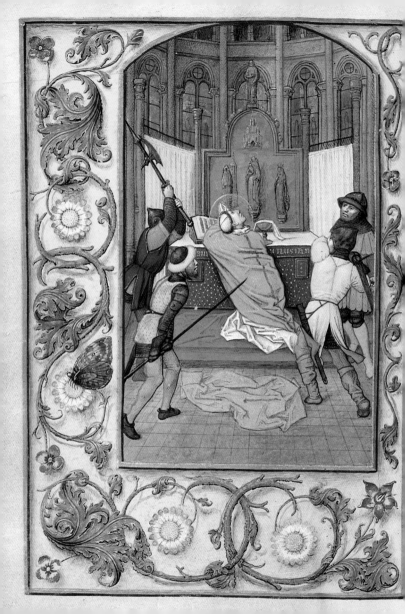

JANUARY

22

23

24

25

26

27

28

St Thomas Becket, f.55v

29

30

31

1

2

3

4

FEBRUARY

5

6

7

8

9

10

11

FEBRUARY

12

13

14

15

16

17

18

19

20

21

22

23

24

25

26

27

28   29 (Leap Year only)

1

2

3

4

MARCH

5

6

7

8

9

10

11

The Virgin and Child, f.59v

12

13

14

15

16

17

18

19

20

21

22

23

24

25

26

27

28

29

30

31

1

St Margaret, f.62v

2

3

4

5

6

7

8

9

10

11

12

13

14

15

APRIL

16

17

18

19

20

21

22

23

24

25

26

27

28

29

30 _____

1 _____

2 _____

3 _____

4 _____

5 _____

6 _____

7

8

9

10

11

12

13

St Sitha, or Zita, of Lucca, f.66v

14

15

16

17

18

19

20

MAY

21

22

23

24

25

26

27

28

29

30

31

1

2

3

Memorial of St Sitha, jousting, f.67

Memoria de sancta sitha. an̄

Aue sancta
famula
sitha ihū
ypī. Que
cum tota
lamma?
deo placuisti. Egenoꝛ et fle
biles de cibo foꝯisti. Cecoꝛ
mutoꝛ debileꝫ et claudos i
uisti. Semper elemosinam
dare quesiuisti. Deum et
ecclesiam virgo dilexisti
fraudem et nequiciam tu
minus odisti. Para nobiꝫ
gloriam quam tu meru

JUNE

4

5

6

7

8

9

10

11

12

13

14

15

16

17

JUNE

18

19

20

21

22

23

24

25

26

27

28

29

30

1

JULY

2

3

4

5

6

7

8

JULY

9

10

11

12

13

14

15

The Annunciation, f.73v

JULY

16

17

18

19

20

21

22

23

24

25

26

27

28

29

30

31

1

2

3

4

5

Matins of the Hours of the Virgin, f.74

Incipiunt hore beatissime
marie virginis secundum
vsum sarum. Ad matitias

Omine la
bia mea a
pries. Et
os meum
annuna
abit lau
dem tuam

Deus in adiutorium
meum intende. Dne
ad adiuuandum me festina
Gloria patri et filio et spi
ritui sancto. Sicut erat in
principio et nunc et semper

AUGUST

6

7

8

9

10

11

12

13

14

15

16

17

18

19

AUGUST

20

21

22

23

24

25

26

27

28

29

30

31

1

2

SEPTEMBER

3

4

5

6

7

8

9

10

11

12

13

14

15

16

D ad sauces.
Eus mad
iutorium
meum intē
de. Domine
ad adiuuā
dum me festina ⸱ Gloria
patri et filio. et spū sancto.
Sicut erat in principio
et nunc et semper et in secula
seculorum Amen. Antiph.

O admirabile ⸱ pnie
omnibus regnauit
decorem indutus est indutꝰ
est dominus fortitudinem
et precinxit se Et tenuit

17

18

19

20

21

22

23

SEPTEMBER

24

25

26

27

28

29

30

1

2

3

4

5

6

7

The Nativity, f.106v

8

9

10

11

12

13

14

15

16

17

18

19

20

21

22

23

24

25

26

27

28

The Annunciation to the Shepherds, f.113v

29

30

31

1

2

3

4

5

6

7

8

9

10

11

12

13

14

15

16

17

18

NOVEMBER

19

20

21

22

23

24

25

26

27

28

29

30

1

2

DECEMBER

3

4

5

6

7

8

9

King David before the Almighty, f.150v

DECEMBER

10

11

12

13

14

15

16

DECEMBER

17

18

19

20

21

22

23

24

25

26

27

28

29

30   31

The Penitential Psalms, f.151

Incipiunt septem psalmi p̄

Dominene
in furore
tuo arguas me neq̄ in ira
tua corripi
as me Miserere mei domine
quoniam infirmus sum sa
na me domine quoniam co̅
turbata sunt omnia ossa
mea Et anima mea tur
bata est valde sed tu domine
vsqz quo Convertere dn̅e
et eripe anima̅ meam sal
uum me fac propter miam

~ A B C ~

Name

Address

Telephone

Fax   Email

Name

Address

Telephone

Fax   Email

Name

Address

Telephone

Fax   Email

Name

Address

Telephone

Fax   Email

Name

Address

Telephone

Fax   Email

~ D E F ~

Name

Address

Telephone

Fax   Email

Name

Address

Telephone

Fax   Email

Name

Address

Telephone

Fax   Email

Name

Address

Telephone

Fax   Email

Name

Address

Telephone

Fax   Email

~ G H I ~

Name

Address

Telephone

Fax   Email

Name

Address

Telephone

Fax   Email

Name

Address

Telephone

Fax   Email

Name

Address

Telephone

Fax   Email

Name

Address

Telephone

Fax   Email

The blessed carried up to heaven, f.230v

~ J K L ~

Name

Address

Telephone

Fax   Email

Name

Address

Telephone

Fax   Email

Name

Address

Telephone

Fax   Email

Name

Address

Telephone

Fax   Email

Name

Address

Telephone

Fax   Email

~ M N O ~

Name

Address

Telephone

Fax   Email

Name

Address

Telephone

Fax   Email

Name

Address

Telephone

Fax   Email

Name

Address

Telephone

Fax   Email

Name

Address

Telephone

Fax   Email

~ P Q R ~

Name

Address

Telephone

Fax   Email

Name

Address

Telephone

Fax   Email

Name

Address

Telephone

Fax   Email

Name

Address

Telephone

Fax   Email

Name

Address

Telephone

Fax   Email

Christ washing the feet of the disciples, f.265v

~ S T ~

Name

Address

Telephone

Fax   Email

Name

Address

Telephone

Fax   Email

Name

Address

Telephone

Fax   Email

Name

Address

Telephone

Fax   Email

Name

Address

Telephone

Fax   Email

~ U V W ~

Name

Address

Telephone

Fax   Email

Name

Address

Telephone

Fax   Email

Name

Address

Telephone

Fax   Email

Name

Address

Telephone

Fax   Email

Name

Address

Telephone

Fax   Email

~ X Y Z ~

Name

Address

Telephone

Fax   Email

Name

Address

Telephone

Fax   Email

Name

Address

Telephone

Fax   Email

Name

Address

Telephone

Fax   Email

Name

Address

Telephone

Fax   Email

St Jerome, f.278v

Border detail from the Psalms of the Passion, f.251

First published 1997 by
The British Library
Great Russell Street, London WC1B 3DG
and
Museums and Galleries Marketing Ltd
24 St Charles Square, London W10 6EE

ISBN 0 7123 4548 5 (BL)
Product code HBDO1 (MGML)

A C K N O W L E D G E M E N T S
Captions and illustrations are selected
from *The Hastings Hours* by Janet Backhouse,
Curator of Illuminated Manuscripts at The British Library
(The British Library and Pomegranate Artbooks, 1996)

Front cover illustration: detail from f.50v
Part-title page illustration: detail from f.66v
Title page illustration: detail from f.65
Back cover illustration: detail from f.73v

Designed and typeset by Roger Davies
Printed in Italy by Artegrafica, Verona

uouum a

oeue mi

stia ut beate elp̄

bue gloriose fa

ra mundi despꝛ